THE
CAT
LOVERS'

POCKET BOOK

The Cat Lovers' Pocket Book

Joan Palmer

Bloomsbury Books · London

First published by Eric Dobby Publishing Ltd.,
12 Warnford Road, Orpington, Kent BR6 6LW.

This edition published by Bloomsbury Books, an imprint of
The Godfrey Cave Group, 42 Bloomsbury Street, London, WC1B 3QJ, 1993

Printed and bound in Great Britain by
BPCC Hazell Books Ltd

Member of BPCC Ltd

ISBN 1 85471 396 5

CONTENTS

Dedication

This book is dedicated to the memory of my late husband, Doug Palmer-Moore, who loved all animals. Also to 'Samson', the Lilac-point Siamese, our devoted – and talkative – companion for fifteen years.

Preface

How many breeds of cats are there? Possibly you can think only of the popular Burmese and Siamese.

There are only two basic body types: the strongly built, rounded headed Persian (Longhair) and the Exotic and British Shorthairs: and the lighter cat with wedge-shaped head as typified by the Siamese, Balinese and other foreign breeds. But there are five coat types, longhair, shorthair, curly, wirehair, even hairless, and various coat patterns and colours.

This book should prove an easy identification guide which will also enable prospective cat buyers to choose the pet that meets their requirements in terms of beauty, character and temperament. There is also a list of useful cat clubs, which the reader may care to join.

No sooner has a cat book been produced with the aim of including every known variety, than another type, or colour of cat, that has been newly developed or is waiting in the wings for acceptance, may be recognised.

It will also be realised that some varieties and/or colours that are accepted for exhibition in the United Kingdom may not be so in the United States and vice-versa. And that there may be some differences in show standards.

Again, one finds in one's research names of cats such as the Supalak or Thong Daeng, ancient Thai breeds which could well have been the ancestors of the Burmese and Havana Brown.

Seychellois are now being developed, described as oriental-type cats with the coat patterns of the Seychelles, and Burmillas which started accidentally through a mismating between Burmese and Chinchilla.

A relatively new approach to developing cat breeds has been the mating of domestic cats with wild cat species. Generally such experimentation results in kittens of wild temperament, but there have been claims in the United States that crossings with Geoffroy's cat *(felis (leopardus) geoffroyi),* found from Bolivia to Patagonia, have proved tame and beautiful, introducing a coat pattern of exotic spots hitherto unknown in domestic cats. One of the names given to these hybrids is Safari cats.

And what of the future? Might I suggest that readers visit a small livestock show and examine the coat patterns of rabbits, mice and cavies? This will enable them to see the direction in which cat breeders could be heading, for gene mutations in our friend, the cat, include those responsible for the coats of fancy-bred animals such as these.

Acknowledgement

I should like to thank my friend, MARC HENRIE, ASC, Photographer of Animals, for allowing me to reproduce his beautiful cat studies in this book.

Marc was working as a Photographer in Hollywood when, one day, he had the chance to photograph famous tough guy star, Edward G Robinson, relaxing by a swimming pool, with his Siamese cat. So successful was the outcome that he was asked to photograph many more celebrities, with their pets, including the inimitable Marilyn Monroe.

Marc now lives in Shepherds Bush, London, with his wife, Fiona, a former dancer, a daughter, Fleur, and numerous pets.

Artwork, Yvonne Dolo, Dolo Designs. Picture of Manx cat, courtesy of Isle of Man Tourism; Domestic and Feral cats, courtesy of the Cats Protection League.

Picture of Snowshoe courtesy of Mrs Maureen Trompetto.

Ancestors of the Cat

The history of the cat can be traced back millions of years to a small, weasel-like creature, the miacis, which was the forerunner of many animals, including bears, civets, dogs and hyenas. The cat family, known as *Felidae*, evolved from the civets.

The domestic cat, in common with the lion, tiger and other big cats, is a member of the *Felidae*, a family of carnivorous mammals made up of three groups, or *genera: Panthera*, the big cats which are able to roar; *Acinonyx*, the Cheetahs which, unlike the other cats cannot retract their claws, and *Felis*, which comprises the remaining cats that are unable to roar.

The domestic cat still closely resembles, and shares a number of characteristics with, the big cats one may see in a safari park or zoo. It has the same rough tongue, the same razor-sharp teeth and, because it walks on its toes, it is able stealthily to stalk its prey. Like the big cats it has retractable claws, cushioned pads and paws, a long, supply body, and a long tail as an aid to balance, except in the case of the tail-less Manx.

Little is known about the first domestic cat. Doubtless, in the same way as wild dogs were enticed, with scraps of meat, to the fireside of early man, small wild cats were fed by humans and gradually became tame. Most likely these early wild cats were the Caffre-Kaffir of Africa which possibly mated with other smaller, wild cats, becoming the ancestors of the pet cats we know today. The Kaffir cat still looks very similar to the popular Abyssinian variety.

There are a number of small, wild cats distributed throughout the world. These include the African Golden cat, Bay cat, Leopard cat, Chinese Desert cat, Caracal, Jungle cat, Pampas cat, Puma or mountain lion, Geoffroy's cat or Ocelot, the Kodkod, Iriomote cat, Mountain cat, African wild cat, Lynx, Pallas's cat, Sand cat, Marbled cat, Black-footed cat, Ocelot, Spanish Lynx, Flat-headed cat, Rusty-spotted cat, Bobcat, Serval, European wild cat, Temminck's Golden cat, Tiger cat, Fishing cat, Margay or Tree Ocelot and the Jaguarundi.

The history of the domestic cat can be traced back more than 4000 years to the time when it was an esteemed pet of the Ancient Egyptians. There are paintings of cats on the walls of Egyptian tombs and statues. Mummified cats have also been found in coffins dating from this period. Cats became the guardians of the granaries by keeping down vermin. Their hunting instincts were put to the test in catching wild fowl for their masters. Over a thousand years ago cats were also known in China, and later Japan, where they kept mice away from silkworm cocoons and priceless manuscripts.

It was, however, the Egyptians who noticed that the pupils of a cat's eyes altered according to the light and that they were extremely fertile. They were therefore credited with magical powers and worshipped at all levels of society. The slaughter of a cat meant severe punishment, even death.

The Egyptians worshipped a number of gods and goddesses, many of which had human shape, but animal heads. The cat was thought to be sacred to the Egyptian goddess Isis. In time it became recognised as an incarnation of deity and it was as the daughter of Isis, and her husband, Osiris, the sun god, that the cat goddess, Bast (Bastet or Pasht) emerged. The word 'puss' derives from Pasht.

Bast was usually represented by a cat's head on a human body. However when the numerous Egyptian gods came into being, the cat was revered for its qualities of ferocity and its prowess as a huntress, so the original statues were lion-headed; although in time Bast became known as a cat-headed goddess, she was always worshipped as a lion-headed deity. Statues in the forms co-existed during the last thousand years of paganism.

In the twenty-second dynasty (*circa* 950 BC) Bast took precedence over all other goddesses becoming known as the Lady of Bubastis.

On an island in the Nile, a large statue, in the likeness of Bast, was erected in the temple of Bubastis to which thousands would travel, by boat, on feast days, so that they might worship. King Osorkon II of Egypt built a magnificent hall in Bubastis which he dedicated to the goddess, and a relief, found on the walls, proclaims his allegiance, thus: 'I give thee every land in obeisance. I give thee all power like Ra (the Sun god)' . . . No wonder the cat has an air of superiority!

When cats died their bodies were mummified. The richer the family of their owners, the more ornate and valuable the coffins would be. Some contained mummified mice so that the cats would not go hungry on their journey to the next world.

The family bereaved of a cat would shave their eyebrows to express their grief. Living cats were zealously guarded, and it was forbidden to take them out of Egypt, though a number did find their way to other lands.

It is generally believed that the first domestic cat came to Britain in the first or second century AD, brought by the invading Romans. The belief is substantiated by footprints in clay tiles and bone discovered in the remains of a Roman villa.

By the tenth century Prince Howel the Wise of Wales had fixed the value of a new born kitten at one penny – a considerable sum in those days. The value was increased when the grown cat had proved its worth as a mouse catcher.

Alas, in the Middle Ages the cat, which had formerly been revered, became an object of fear, even hatred, because of its association with black magic and witchcraft. Indeed many harmless men and women were condemned as witches, or wizards, simply because they kept a harmless pet cat. It seemed a strange way of repaying the animal which had proved itself the friend of man by helping to combat the brown rat, which brought the Black Death, or Bubonic Plague, to Britain, virtually wiping out half of London, in 1766, prior to the Great Fire of London.

Thankfully, the cat regained popularity in the Victorian age. It became known as a clean animal that destroyed vermin and many a shopkeeper kept one for this purpose. It also represented the most desirable traits of Victorian family life, for the queen cat had large litters and was a good mother. And so it began to be portrayed on post cards, chocolate boxes and samplers. There were cat-like ornaments in abundance, and the cat even became a popular pantomime figure, featured in such productions as *Puss and Boots* and *Dick Whittington and his Cat.*

Perhaps not generally know is that the story of Dick Whittington and his cat is not sheer fantasy, for Richard (Dick) Whittington (*circa* 1358-1423), the third son of Sir William Whittington of Pauntley, Gloucester, did indeed marry Alice Fitzwarren and became Lord Mayor of London. But Dick was not, as the pantomime would have us believe, a poor boy, and it is not known if he did own a cat.

However, the Reverend Samuel Lyons, an accredited biographer of Whittington, writes of a fifteenth century figure of a boy, with a cat, discovered at a house in Gloucester once occupied by the Whittington family; and, according to the historian William Maitland, when the infamous Newgate Prison was rebuilt, following the Great Fire of London there was found amidst the ruins a figure of a boy with the word *Libertas* carved on his hat, and a companion cat at his feet.

Visitors to Holloway, north of London may see the famous Whittington Stone where Dick is said to have sat in despair, until the Bow Bells rang out, urging him: 'Turn again, Whittington, Lord Mayor of London.' And on nearby Highgate Hill there is a statue of Dick's cat. Both are charming reminders of a fascinating tale and cause many a busy passer-by to stop and ponder.

Cat Varieties

In the following pages you will find photographs and descriptions of more than one hundred beautiful cats. In some cases there may be a photograph without accompanying copy. This is because the picture is of but another colour variation of a cat that has been previously described. There are not, for instance, as many varieties of pure bred cats as there are pure bred dogs, but new colour patterns have gradually been introduced.

In writing about exhibiting cats I will explain how new cat breeds are established. However, for the benefit of this section, let me explain that, cats are basically divided into two main types; cats with long fur, whose ancestors came from Ankara (then called Angora) in Turkey, and Iran (then called Persia), and those with short fur.

The cats with short coats are, however, again divided thus:

Those with short fur, round heads, big rounded eyes and shortish thick tails, known as BRITISH cats (said to be descended from the cats that came with the Romans);

FOREIGN (Oriental) short-hairs with longish heads, almond-shaped eyes, and long thin tails, which came in the first place from cats brought from the Far East;

SIAMESE of similar shape, but having pale fur on their bodies and dark faces, ears, legs and tails;

REX, Slim cats, unusual in that the fur is very short and curly.

It is general practice in the UK to refer to all Persian colour varieties simply as Longhairs, for instance, Bi-Colour Longhair. In America however they are listed as varieties of Persian.

Genetically, short-coats are dominant to long-coats, so most 'pet' cats are short-coated. It is also the fact

17

that while many, but not all, ginger cats are toms, that is male, virtually all tortoiseshell cats are female.

CAT
BREEDS

Abyssinian (Blue)

Characteristics: A gentle, playful cat. It is loving and kind with children.

Origin: A Mrs Burrett-Lennard is credited with bringing a cat from Abyssinia (Ethiopia) to the UK in 1868. This could well have been the ancestor of the breed we know today. Abyssinians are very popular in North America. However all American Abyssinians trace back to British imported stock.

Grooming: See Abyssinian (Ruddy).

Breeding: See Abyssinian (Ruddy).

Colouring: Soft, warm, blue-grey body ticked with deeper steel blue; undercoat pale cream or oatmeal. Belly and inside legs pale cream or oatmeal as undercoat. Spinal shading should be a deeper colour. Tail tip and solid colour on hind legs, steel blue. Nose leather dark pink. Pads, mauve or blue.

NB: Silver, lilac, chocolate and cream are just some of the Abyssinian colours which are being achieved.

Desired qualities: An alert, athletic cat with a foreign head shape. Not so elongated as that of the Siamese.

Drawbacks: None known.

Abyssinian (Ruddy)

Characteristics: Intelligent, obedient and fond of human company. Can be taught to perform tricks. Energetic, with a dislike of being confined, the Abyssinian is not the ideal 'apartment' cat.

Origin: One of the oldest breeds with a striking resemblance to the sacred cats of Ancient Egypt, Abyssinians were once known as 'Rabbit' or 'Hare' cats – their ticked coats bear a resemblance to these animals. 'Zula', a cat brought to the United Kingdom from Abyssinia (Ethiopia) at the end of the Abyssinian War (1860s), was doubtless bred from with a cat of similar markings.

Grooming: Stroking improves coat. Use a soft bristled brush and a fine-toothed comb to remove loose hairs. Rubbing with a chamois leather makes the coat shine.

Breeding: Litters average four. Kittens bear a fluffy coat, with dark markings which disappear as they reach maturity.

Colouring: Ruddy is the 'normal' coat colour. A rich, golden brown ticked with black or dark brown. Pale orange-brown undercoat. Eyes: amber, hazel or green.

Desired qualities: A medium-sized oriental-type cat with an alert, lively appearance.

Drawbacks: None known. But the Abyssinian does prefer country life. (It is a breed often favoured by men!)

Abyssinian – Sorrel (Red)

Characteristics: The Abyssinian enjoys human company. Like the Burmese and Siamese, it may be trained to the lead. An active cat whose freedom should not be curtailed.

Origin: Some claim that the Abyssinian's origins may be traced to the Nile Valley. It certainly resembles the sacred cats of Ancient Egypt.

Grooming: See Abyssinian (Ruddy).

Breeding: The Abyssinian queen usually has smaller litters, about four, than other oriental breeds. A quiet cat, the Abyssinian queen does not call loudly, when on heat.

Colouring: The Red Abyssinian (called Sorrel in the UK and Canada) has a body colour of copper red, ticked with chocolate. Paler, deep apricot undercoat, spinal shading of a deeper colour. Tail tip, and edges of ears, chocolate. Nose leather and pads pinks.

Desired qualities: Darker colouring up the back of hind legs. Ear tufts admired.

Drawbacks: None known.

American Shorthair

Characteristics: Friendly, hardy, companionable and fearless. Likes its freedom and is a good hunter.

Origin: Believed to have arrived in America with European settlers. Many were ships' cats whose job it was to protect provisions. They abandoned ship and mated with local stock, the resultant progeny developing their own characteristics. Otherwise similar to British shorthairs, the American is a larger cat with a less rounded head and longer nose.

Grooming: Easy to look after. Regular combing.

Breeding: Rarely have problems. Kittens have strong sense of preservation and are generally healthy.

Colouring: More than thirty colour patterns at recent count. New colours frequently being introduced. Popular colours include black, blue, red, chinchilla, cream, bicolour and lovely smokey tabby and calico shades.

Desired qualities: A largish cat with a thick, short, even coat; a medium-length tail, ears set wide apart and large, round eyes with 'wide-awake' expression.

Drawbacks: None known.

American Wirehair

Characteristics: Like its Shorthair counterpart, the American Wirehair is good natured, robust and, with its thick, sheep-like coat, is an interesting pet to own. Breed members are, alas, not all that easy to obtain.

Origin: First recorded at Verona, New York in 1966, occurring in a normal-coated shorthaired litter.

Grooming: Regular, gentle brushing with a soft brush to remove loose hairs. Shampoo before exhibition.

Breeding: All American Wirehairs trace back to the original mutant, Adam, and a wirehair mating with normal-coated shorthairs will produce 50% wirehair kittens.

Colouring: See American Shorthair. But not chocolate, lilac and Himalayan.

Desired qualities: A medium-sized cat with a tightly curled coat, not unlike that of a lamb.

Drawbacks: None known – except difficulty in obtaining a kitten.

Angora

Characteristics: Quiet, friendly and adaptable. Loves to have an audience. Owners sometimes learn to spin the hair from its long, silky coat.

Origin: One of the oldest long-haired cats in Europe, the Angora, which originates in Ankara, Turkey, was introduced into France, in the 16th century, by naturalist, Nicholas Claude Fabri de Peirese. At the end of that century, some Angoras came to Britain. For a time they were known as French cats.

Grooming: Daily use of a medium-toothed comb and removal of dead hairs. (Sheds in spring and summer.)

Breeding: Litters usually number four or five. Kittens are slow developers. It could be at least two years before youngsters display a long, silky coat.

Colouring: White is the usual colour, but all longhair cat colours are accepted. These include black, blue, chocolate in self and tabby patterns.

Desired qualities: A medium-sized cat that is solid, lithe and graceful. It should have a long, flowing silky coat and a medium-sized head, wide, with gently pointed wedge.

Drawbacks: Deafness not unusual.

Balinese (Siamese Longhair)

Characteristics: Lively. Not as vocal as the usual Siamese. Affectionate, dislikes being along, and generally good with children.

Origin: First appeared in litters in the USA deriving from Siamese with a mutant gene for longhair. Selective breeding resulted in recognition of the breed in 1963 – by all governing bodies in the USA by 1970. The name Balinese was bestowed because of the breed's graceful movements, said to be like those of a Balinese dancer.

Grooming: Use a soft brush to remove dead hairs.

Breeding: Balinese breed true, but occasional outcrossing to Siamese (Shorthair) improves type.

Colouring: All Siamese colours accepted in the UK, but only seal, chocolate, blue and lilac in the USA, where other Siamese colours are described as Javanese and the cats known as Javanese rather than Balinese cats.

Desired qualities: A medium-sized, dainty cat with an ermine-like soft, silky coat, and medium-sized almond eyes which slant towards the nose.

Drawbacks: None known.

28

Bicolour Persian

Characteristics: Beautiful and unusual. A quiet cat that lends itself to apartment living. Docile and affectionate. Hates being teased.

Origin: There have been longhaired cats in Europe since the 16th century. There were two types: the Angora, which came from Turkey, the Persian, which came from Persia (now Iran). Both types could have originated in Russia, where their long coat would have given protection against severe weather conditions.

Grooming: Daily use of a wide-toothed comb, then a fine-toothed one to remove dead hairs. Finally, use a pure bristle brush. Check eyes for staining.

Breeding: Queens usually produce three or four kittens. Bicolour will beget bicolour. So will mating a bicolour with a tortoiseshell and white, and bicolour with a solid colour, or a solid colour with a white.

Colouring: Black and white, blue and white, red and white, and cream and white.

Desired qualities: A patched cat with not more than two thirds of the body coloured, not more than one-half white. Nose leather and paws are generally pink, eyes deep copper or orange.

Drawbacks: Moults.

Birman (sacred cat of Burma)

Characteristics: Lively, intelligent and affectionate. Not as placid as the Persian, nor as keyed up as the Siamese.

Origin: The original Birmans are said to have been a gift to France from the priest of the Temple of Lao-Tsun in Tibet, where they were temple cats. Other sources would have it that they were produced in France by mating Siamese cats with longhaired black and white cats.

Grooming: Daily grooming with a soft brush. Not so difficult to keep tangle free as the Persian.

Breeding: Mate as early as seven months. Litters usually number three to five. Kittens are born white. Colour points become visible within a few days. Eyes are baby blue before developing to normal adult colour.

Colouring: Seal-point, chocolate-point, blue-point and lilac-point.

Desired qualities: A body that is large and low on the legs, but longer than that of the Persian or Himalayan. Mask, ears, legs and tail of correct contrasting colour.

Drawbacks: None known.

Bombay

Characteristics: An attractive, good-tempered cat, easy to look after, and usually reliable with children and other pets.

Origin: Produced by crossing Brown Burmese with Black American Shorthairs. It is said that the Bombay has inherited the toughness of the American and the delightful temperament of the Burmese.

Grooming: Daily combing. An occasional polish with chamois leather. Stroking improves coat.

Breeding: Despite its hybrid ancestry, the Bombay breeds true.

Colouring: Black from root to tip without white hairs or patches. Eyes usually copper; occasionally gold.

Desired qualities: The most important aspect of this variety is its coat, which should be close-lying with a sheen like that of the Burmese.

Drawbacks: Like the Burmese, it has a strong personality and enjoys plenty of attention.

Blue-Cream Persian

Characteristics: Beautiful, affectionate, quiet. Easily adaptable to apartment life.

Origin: Have appeared in litters from blue and cream matings since early days of cat shows and were shown in the USA as Blue Tortoiseshells in the 1900s. They received recognition in the UK in 1930.

Grooming: Daily brushing and combing. This colour benefits from bathing and powdering before a show.

Breeding: A blue male mated to a cream female will produce blue-cream females and cream male kittens. Blue-creams are a female-only variety.

Colouring: An evenly-coloured coat in pastel shades of blue and cream. Eyes, deep copper or orange. Americans like the coat blue patched with solid cream, well defined, broken on body, face, legs and tail.

Desired qualities: See Colouring. (American and UK show standards vary quite widely.)

Drawbacks: None known.

British Bicolour Shorthair

Characteristics: Unusual two-coloured cat that is generally hardy, intelligent and affectionate.

Origin: Have been in evidence for centuries but only received recognition for show purposes fairly recently after their usefulness in producing other colours became apparent (see Breeding).

Grooming: Daily combing. Stroking improves coat.

Breeding: Bicolours are necessary in the breeding of tortoiseshell and whites and dilute calico. May result from matings between self coloured males and tortoishell and white females, between bicolour males and tortoiseshell and white females, and between two bicolours or a self coloured and a white cat.

Colouring: A coat pattern like that of a Dutch rabbit with symmetrical patches of colour, either black, blue, red or cream, evenly distributed on head, body and tail.

33

Desired qualities: A shorthair whose coat should be not more than two-thirds coloured and not more than half should be white. A white facial blaze is desirable. Eyes: brilliant copper or orange.

Drawbacks: None, except difficulty in obtaining one of required show standard.

British Black

Characteristics: Healthy cat. Much sought after because of its association with 'good luck'. Usually an expert hunter, yet affectionate and good with other pets.

Origin: See Cat Varieties. A natural breed and, in the case of the Black, one with a chequered history; on the one hand having been reviled as the witches' 'familiar', linked with evil doing, and on the other, as the bringer of 'good fortune', particularly in the UK when it 'crosses our path'. Superstitions still abound and vary from country to country.

Grooming: Daily combing. Rubbing the coat with bay rum will make it shine.

Breeding: Black cat mated to black cat will produce like offspring. May also appear in tortoiseshell litters.

Colouring: Jet black, glossy coat. Eyes pure copper (or orange). No greeny tinge after kittenhood.

Desired qualities: Medium to large cat that is strong, sturdy and has short legs.

Drawbacks: None known.

British Blue

Characteristics: Popular and attractive, the British Blue has an equable temperament and is much in demand as both pet and show exhibit.

Origin: Self blue cats have appeared in most countries of the world. There are more in Scandinavia than in the UK. Some say that the British Blue is identical with the French Chartreux, but the fur of the latter is thought to be more greyish-blue.

Grooming: Daily combing. Rub down with a silk handkerchief. Stroking makes the coat gleam.

Breeding: Breed true. However, outcrossing with shorthaired blacks or longhaired blues is said to improve quality.

Colouring: Light- to medium-blue coat. Eyes, copper or orange.

Desired qualities: A chubby body, with smooth plush-like fur, and a gentle placid temperament.

Drawbacks: None known.

British Blue-Cream Shorthair

Characteristics: See British Blue and British Cream. Like the British Tortoiseshell Shorthair, it is a female-only variety.

Origin: Although, for many years, Blue-Cream kittens had appeared in litters resulting from blue and cream matings, they were not recognised as a variety in the UK prior to 1956.

Grooming: Daily combing. Before a show, an application of bay rum to the coat works wonders.

Breeding: Produced by mating a Blue with a Cream Shorthair, or from tortoiseshells. However it is not possible to breed blue-creams where a blue-cream female is mated to a cream sire.

Colouring: Blue and cream in a pastel shade, preferably without a red tinge.

Desired qualities: Blue and cream pastel coat without a facial blaze. Eyes, copper or orange.

Drawbacks: None known. But not easy to determine this colour variety at birth.

British Cream

Characteristics: A rare and charming variety that has all the best characteristics of British shorthairs, but is not easy to breed without tabby markings.

Origin: Creams occasionally appeared in tortoiseshell litters, but were not recognised as a variety in their own right and admitted for competition until the late 1920s.

Grooming: Daily combing. Stroking will improve coat. May need a bath a few days prior to exhibition.

Breeding: Difficult to breed without tabby markings. A cream male can be produced by mating a blue-cream to a blue sire; females by mating a blue-cream to a cream sire.

Colouring: Light even colour without any sign of white. Eyes should be copper or orange.

Desired qualities: Good broad head, small ears, and big eyes.

Drawbacks: Rarity, and difficulty in breeding.

British Smoke Shorthair

Characteristics: Affectionate and healthy, usually good with other pets and requiring little grooming.

Origin: Appeared from time to time in litters of blacks and blues. British Smoke Shorthairs are the counterpart of Persian Smokes and have a similar history. They now warrant show classes after, for some while, being restricted to AOV (Any other Variety).

Grooming: Daily combing. Stroking improves coat. Powdering, or shampooing, a few days before a show, if considered necessary.

Breeding: Obtained by mating Silver Tabby Shorthairs to solid-coloured Shorthairs. Thereafter, breed Smoke to Smoke and, occasionally, to Blues to gain quality.

Colouring: Black or blue. Undercoat pale silver. Eyes, yellow or orange.

Desired qualities: See Cat Varieties. Nose leather, and pads, should be blue or black to correspond with coat colour.

Drawbacks: None known.

British Tabby Shorthair

Characteristics: An attractive, striped cat with markings that have been apparent since the days of the Ancient Egyptians. Usually a healthy, contented cat that makes a good household pet.

Origin: The name 'Tabby' originates from the likeness of the cat's coat pattern to tabby silk. The word comes from Attabiya, the area of Baghdad where the material was made. However, striped, or spotted cats were also depicted on Ancient Egyptian scrolls. They have also been known as Cyprus cats.

Grooming: Daily grooming. An application of bay rum makes the coat shine.

Breeding: Breed true. Occasional outcrossing may improve type.

Colouring: The classic tabby pattern has a characteristic head-marking like the letter 'M' on the forehead. Unbroken lines run from the outer corners of the eyes towards the back of

head and there should be other pencillings on
the cheeks. Lines extend from top of head to the
shoulder markings. Three unbroken lines run
parallel to each other down the spine. Tabby
patterns include mackerel, spotted, brown, red,
silver, blue and cream.

Desired qualities: See Cat Varieties.

Drawbacks: None known.

British Tipped Shorthair

Characteristics: Rare and striking variety that has a white undercoat tipped with a contrasting colour. They are happy, hardy cats and make good pets.

Origin: The shorthaired counterpart of longhaired Chinchillas, Cameos and Shaded Silvers and Cameos, with a similar background.

Grooming: Daily combing. Occasional powdering.

Breeding: Usually derived from the mating of a Silver Tabby shorthair to a Chinchilla, then back to Chinchilla Shorthairs. There have, however, been many unexpected crosses.

Colouring: Tipping may be any colour but undercoat should be as white as possible. Tabby markings are a fault.

Desired qualities: A shorthaired cat, the top coat of which should be tipped on the back, flanks, head, ears, legs and tail with a contrasting colour. Eyes, green in black tipped cats, orange or copper in other colours.

Drawbacks: None known.

British Tortoiseshell Shorthair

Characteristics: See Cat Varieties. Tortoiseshell cats are almost always sweet-natured and, although there are exceptions, are almost always female.

Origin: Tortoiseshell cats, which have great charm, have been known and exhibited ever since cat shows began.

Grooming: See other British Shorthairs.

Breeding: Because tortoiseshells are inevitably female, it is necessary to mate the tortie to a solid coloured male of the desired colour, usually cream, red, or black.

Colouring: Black with brilliant patches of cream and red. All patches must be clearly defined, well broken on legs and body.

Desired qualities: See British Shorthair. A red or cream blaze on head is desirable. Eyes, brilliant copper or orange.

Drawbacks: None known.

British Tortoiseshell and White Shorthair

Characteristics: A female-only variety with all the best British Shorthair characteristics. Usually very affectionate.

Origin: Once known as Chintz (Spanish cats) they have been known for centuries and described as 'alley' cats, despite their brilliant coloured coat patches.

Grooming: See British Tortoiseshell Shorthair.

Breeding: Bicolours have been found to be the best sires, particularly if from a tortie and white mother.

Colouring: The coat should be brilliantly patched with black, cream and red, but with additional areas of white. Patches should cover top of head, ears, back and tail, also part of the sides. A white forehead blaze is desirable. Eyes, copper or orange.

Desired qualities: Bold colouring as described, in which white must not predominate.

Drawbacks: None known.

44

British White

Characteristics: Very clean, affectionate cat, often of high intelligence and generally healthy.

Origin: Natural breed (see British Shorthair) yet relatively rare. Regarded as a symbol of purity in some countries, in particular, Japan. There is a Buddhist belief that having a light coloured cat ensures that there will always be silver in the house (the black cat signifies gold!).

Grooming: Daily grooming. Before a show, brush baby powder through the coat or use a baby shampoo. There should be no yellow tinge in the coat.

Breeding: There are in fact three varieties of the White Shorthair, only the eye colours differing. Eyes may be blue (intense sapphire), orange, or there may be one eye deep blue, the other orange (only non-pedigree white cats have green eyes). They may be mated white to white, or used with tortoiseshells to yield tortoiseshell and white, or with solid colours to produce bicolours.

Colouring: A pure white coat without any yellow tinge (see note on eye colours).

Desired qualities: Medium – to large-sized cat with short legs and a short, thick coat.

Drawbacks: Deafness may occur in blue-eyed whites and, in the case of the odd-eyed white, deafness may occur on the blue side.

Burmese

Characteristics: One of the most popular
pedigree cats. Affectionate, beautiful, intelligent,
playful, and easy to train.

Origin: Cats similar to the Burmese were
recorded in Thailand as early as the 15th
century. However, it was not until 1930 when a
brown oriental-type cat named Wong Mau was
imported to the west coast of America that
development of the breed began. Wong Mau was
mated to a Siamese, but when the kittens were
mated back to their mother brown kittens
resulted. The first brown Burmese reached the
UK in 1948. Now the Burmese rivals the
Siamese in popularity stakes.

Grooming: Use a fine-toothed comb. Stroking
helps the coat and so does a bran bath, which
will absorb any grease.

Breeding: A Burmese queen may have as many as
ten kittens, though this is the exception, not the
rule.

Colouring: While brown is the original, and most popular colour, Burmese are bred in blue, chocolate, lilac, red, cream, brown tortie, blue tortie, chocolate tortie and lilac tortie.

Desired qualities: A medium-sized cat, hard and muscular with golden-yellow eyes.

Drawbacks: None known.

Chartreuse

The Chartreuse was once a much bigger cat than the British Blue. Now they have the same show standard and are identical.

Characteristics: The Chartreuse (Chartreux) is a French cat almost identical in looks and character to the British Blue.

Origin: Said to have been brought to France from South Africa by the monks of the Order of Chartreux, the variety has had many famous owners, including the French novelist, Colette.

Grooming: See British Blue.

Breeding: Breeds true, but see British Blue.

Colouring: Greyish-blue.

Desired qualities: Like the British Blue, but the head is less rounded, and the chest is deeper.

Drawbacks: None known. A most attractive cat.

Chinchilla

Characteristics: One of the most popular longhairs. Dainty yet hardy, with mystical expression and as loving as it is healthy.

Origin: One of the first man-made varieties believed to have evolved from Silver Tabbies. Early exhibits were said to have derived from Silver and Blue Tabby crosses.

Grooming: Hard work if you plan to exhibit. Bath about a week before a show, then powder daily to restore the coat's body. Comb to prevent tangles The cat should be fluffy with each hair standing out. Make sure all traces of powder are removed.

Breeding: Usually produce three or four kittens. But best not to mate the queen until she is at least twelve months old. Kittens often exhibit tabby markings and rings on the tail. These usually fade as they mature.

Colouring: Undercoat pure white. The coat on back, flanks, head, ears and tail, tipped with brown, which should be evenly distributed. Nose-tip, brick-red. Skin on eyelids and pads, black or dark brown.

Desired qualities: A dainty looking cat, smaller in physique than other longhairs yet compact and cobby with body set low on short, sturdy legs.

Drawbacks: Needs lots of grooming.

Colourpoint Longhair (Himalayan)

Characteristics: Beautiful, intelligent. Makes a fine family pet, despite its love of freedom.

Origin: The Colourpoint is a Persian with Siamese (or Himalayan) colouring that was breeder-designed. This is not a longhaired Siamese, but rather a Persian with Siamese colouring. The description Himalayan comes from the coat pattern of the Himalayan rabbit, the darker colour of which is restricted to the face, legs and tail – like, in fact, the Siamese!

Grooming: Regular grooming with a wide-toothed comb to remove knots. Use a medium-toothed comb for removing dead hairs. Brushing should follow.

Breeding: Breeds true, but outcrosses to self coloured Persians, whose kittens are mated back to original colourpoints, are said to preserve type.

Colouring: All point colours as in the Siamese.

Desired qualities: A cat that is cobby and low on the legs, deep in the chest and massive across the shoulders and rump. Svelte Siamese lines are a fault

Drawbacks: None known. However fairly expensive.

Colourpoint Shorthair

Characteristics: See Siamese.

Origin: This is basically a Siamese cat the point colours of which differ from the usual seal, chocolate, lilac and blue. They have resulted from out crossing Siamese to shorthaired cats of the desired colours.

Grooming: See Siamese.

Breeding: See Origin. These cats are regarded as Siamese in most countries of the world, except in the USA where their classification is as Colourpoint Shorthair.

Colouring: There are many colours, including red-point, cream-point, seal tortie-point, chocolate tortiepoint, blue-cream point and blue and lilac tabby-point.

Desired qualities: The main contrasting colour should, as in the Siamese, be confined to the points: mask, ears, legs and tail.

Drawbacks: None known.

Cornish Rex

Characteristics: Intelligent. An affectionate cat that 'may' wag its tail when it is pleased. (So may the Devon Rex!) Always an attention-getter because of its curly coat, another plus is that it can sometimes be trained to the harness and lead.

Origin: There are two types of Rex cats, the Cornish and the Devon. This is the original mutation, first found in Cornwall, England, in 1950. Early Rexes were outcrossed to British shorthairs. Since 1965 breeders have aimed for 'foreign' type.

Grooming: Easy. Polish with a silk cloth or chamois leather. Lots of stroking! Bath a couple of weeks before an exhibition.

Breeding: Mating of Cornish Rex to Cornish Rex will produce Rex-coated kittens. They are almost always healthy – and hyper-active.

Colouring: Most colour and coat patterns acceptable, including the Himalayan (Si-Rex)

pattern. In the UK any white marking should be
symmetrical (except in tortoiseshell and white).

Desired qualities: A cat that resembles the sacred
cat of Ancient Egypt. The coat forms waves over
the body. Head, body, legs and tail are
proportionately long.

Drawbacks: Inclined to greed.

Cream Persian

Characteristics: Rare, ethereal-looking cat with a sweet temperament and long, flowing coat.

Origin: First recorded in the UK in 1890. At that time thought of as reds, too pale to meet the exhibition standard. Many were sold as pets or exported. Possibly Cream Persians first appeared in litters born to tortoiseshells which had been mated to red tabby males.

Grooming: Daily grooming. Powdering before a show, and an application of bay rum, improves coat.

Breeding: Usually produced from matings of blues and creams. A cream male mated to a blue female will produce cream kittens. The faint tabby markings in kittens gradually fades.

Colouring: A cream coat without markings of any other colour, the coat should be the same colour from root to tip.

Desired qualities: The typical cobby body, short tail and broad head of the Persion cat.

Drawbacks: Not very plentiful, possibly because they have small litters.

Cymric (Longhaired Manx)

Characteristics: Affectionate, intelligent, quiet and loyal. Its unusual appearance is bound to be a talking point.

Origin: Manx breeders in North America were delighted when, in the 1960s, tail-less kittens, with long hair began to appear. The Manx had never been knowingly outcrossed to a long haired cat but the recessive gene for long hair had obviously been inherited from shorthairs without tails used as outcrosses in the past. It was found that the Cymrics, as they were called, bred true.

Grooming: Daily combing.

Breeding: The mating of Cymric to Cymric produces like kittens. However, it is thought that best results are obtained by mating tail-less cats to 'Stumpies'.

Colouring: All colour coats and combinations are accepted with the exception of chocolate, lilac and the Himalayan pattern, or these colours with white.

Desired qualities: A Manx cat, with a smooth, medium long coat, and tufted ears and jowls.

Drawbacks: None known (but see Manx).

Devon Rex

Characteristics: Mischievous, intelligent and affectionate. Like the Cornish Rex it has a curly coat, but its face is wider and more pixieish.

Origin: The second Rex mutation that appeared in 1960. Matings to Cornish Rex queens produced straight-coated progeny proving the two mutations to be dissimilar. Perpetuated by back-crossing the first filial generation to the sire. Of 'foreign' type but the head is full cheeked, with a whisker break. (The nose of the Cornish Rex is more Roman.)

Grooming: See Cornish Rex.

Breeding: Breeds true. The queens make excellent mothers.

Colouring: Most colours and coat patterns acceptable. These include the Himalayan (Si-Rex) coat pattern. White markings are unacceptable in the UK (except in tortoishell and white. At the time of writing, chocolate, lilac and Si-Rex are not acceptable in the USA.

Desired qualities: Similar in build to the Cornish Rex. A medium-sized cat with long tail and huge ears, but with a coarser coat than its counterpart. Many say that it is more playful!

Drawbacks: Rather too fond of food for the good of its waistline!

Domestic Pet Cat (Household cat)

Characteristics: Adaptable, affectionate, hardy and intelligent. Usually a good hunter.

Origin: The Pet (Household) cat has the same common ancestry as the purebred cat, but without the benefit of selective breeding does not conform to any required show standard.

Grooming: Brushing and combing daily will keep the fur clean and shining.

Breeding: Most conscientious owners of non-pedigree cats have the tom (male) cat neutered and the queen spayed. The queen comes into season every three or four weeks in summer and there are never enough homes to go round. The tom unlike the confined, pure-bred stud cat will, if undoctored, become a compulsive fighter and is likely to become injured.

Colouring: Any colour or coat pattern.

Desired qualities: The pet (household) cat may have a coat of any length and colour pattern. Its eyes are usually green or yellow, its nose fairly long.

Drawbacks: None known. You would be doing the cat a favour by adopting it.

Egyptian Mau

Characteristics: Quiet, friendly, playful, good with children. Easy to look after.

Origin: Said to be blessed with a good memory, the Egyptian Mau originated in Cairo and is believed to be a descendant of cats worshipped by the Ancient Egyptians. The name 'Mau' is the Egyptian word for cat. Spotted cats of this type are depicted in Ancient Egyptian art. Breed members appeared at a Cat Show in Rome in the mid-1950s. They were taken to the USA in 1956.

Grooming: Easy to look after. Benefit from regular brushing. Remove all dead hairs from coat.

Breeding: Usually four in a litter. Can be more. Kittens are born with the spots they will carry through life. Queens are generally good mothers.

Colouring: Silver (black spots on agouti background), bronze (chocolate spots on bronze agouti), smoke (black spots on grey, with silver undercoat). Eyes should be pale 'gooseberry'!

Desired qualities: The forehead of this cat is barred with 'M' and frown marks, the cheeks with 'mascara' lines. Shoulder markings are described as a transition between stripes and spots.

Drawbacks: None known.

Exotic Shorthair

Characteristics: A quiet, playful cat, good with children and having all the attributes of a short-haired Persian.

Origin: Man-designed to comply with the wish of some breeders to produce a Persian-type cat with a short coat.

Grooming: Daily combing with a medium toothed comb.

Breeding: To be acknowledged as an Exotic Shorthair, one parent must be Persian, the other an American Shorthair. Alternatively, both may be Exotic Shorthair.

Colouring: All colours and coat patterns within the American Shorthair and Persian are allowed.

Desired qualities: See Persian. But with a short, plush coat. Eyes should be large, round, full and set wide apart.

Drawbacks: Rarity in the UK.

Feral cat

Characteristics: The feral cat is a domestic cat turned wild. It is sometimes possible, with perseverance and patience, to renew its trust in humans.

Origin: The abandoned household cat will eventually become what is known as feral, or half wild, living in a group of cats, usually based on mother-kitten units. Animal welfare workers try to trap such cats and have them neutered in an effort to prevent the ever-growing feral cat population.

Grooming: The cats keep themselves relatively clean.

Breeding: Every effort is made to neuter feral packs. The feral cat is distinguishable from the European wild cat by its pointed tail-tip and smaller head.

Colouring: After several generations of living wild, cats tend to revert to tabby coat patterns.

Desired qualities: Not applicable.

Drawbacks: The cats are in danger of extermination by various authorities if numbers are not kept down by neutering campaigns.

Havana (Havana Brown)

Characteristics: Beautiful, intelligent, playful and devoted to its human family. Happiest around people.

Origin: Cats with all-brown coats were treasured in their native Siam where they were said to protect their owners from evil. They were among the first Siamese-type cats to arrive in the West. However, the Havana Brown was so named because of the likeness of its coat colour to a Havana cigar. The variety was developed by mating a seal-point Siamese with a domestic shorthair. However while British Havanas were bred back to Siamese to keep oriental type, this was not permitted in the USA.

Grooming: Daily combing with a fine-toothed comb. Polish with a chamois leather before exhibition.

Breeding: Kittens are born with the same coat colour they will carry through life, but lacking the adult sheen. White hairs disappear in adulthood.

Colouring: A rich, warm, chocolate brown. Eyes are pale-to mid-green.

Desired qualities: A medium-sized cat of solid colour and firm muscles. Coat should be medium length, and tail medium length, tapering to a point, without kinks.

Drawbacks: Only its need for love and attention.

Japanese Bobtail

Characteristics: Intelligent and friendly with a distinctive short, bobbed tail, the Japanese Bobtail (or Mi-Ke cat) loves swimming and retrieves like a dog. Has an endearing habit of standing with a front paw uplifted in welcome.

Origin: A native of Japan the Bobtail is a natural breed likenesses of which have decorated temples and appeared in paintings for centuries.

Grooming: Gentle brushing and combing. A pure-bristle brush and medium-toothed comb is recommended.

Breeding: Matings of Bobtail to Bobtail breed true.

Colouring: The more brilliant and bizarre the better. The Himalayan pattern and Abyssinian (unpatterned agouti) are not allowed.

Desired qualities: Medium-sized, slender and shapely, with a decidedly Japanese set to the eyes.

Drawbacks: None known.

Korat

Characteristics: A sweet, gentle cat with an appealing, heart-shaped face. It is affectionate, playful and becomes greatly attached to its human family.

Origin: Prized in Thailand, where it has been known for hundreds of years – it is known in the town of Korat as 'Si-Sawat' (which means good fortune) – the lucky cat found its way to the UK via the US in 1972. Legend has it that a breed member was show at the National Cat Club Shown in 1896, but at the time it was thought to be a Blue Siamese!

Grooming: Daily combing. Polish with a chamois leather. Lots of stroking!

Breeding: Every effort is being made to keep the breed pure. Kittens are born with the beautiful silver-grey coat that they will carry through life.

Colouring: Silver-blue all over. Paw pads, dark blue or lavender with a pinkish hue. Eyes, brilliant green, with an amber tinge allowed in kittens.

Desired qualities: A medium-sized, strong muscular cat, the male being more powerful than the queen.

Drawbacks: Greatly upset by sudden noises.

Maine Coon

Characteristics: A big, hardy cat that is adaptable and affectionate. Although longhaired, it does not need a great deal of grooming.

Origin: Likely to have evolved through crossings between shorthaired cats of settlers and Angoras brought by sailors from the east. Possibly the name 'Coon' was bestowed because of the cat's similarity to the racoon.

Grooming: The Maine Coon has an almost short coat at the front, but a longhaired back and stomach. It does not need as much grooming as other longhairs. A brush and comb every few days should suffice.

Breeding: The Mane Coon queen has only one litter a year, which may have many coat patterns.

Colouring: All coat colours and patterns and combinations of colours and patterns are acceptable. The colour standard is the same as for Persian cats.

Desired qualities: A big strong cat with a rugged coat and a head that is small in proportion to the body, set on a medium-sized, powerful neck.

Drawbacks: None known.

Manx

Characteristics: An affectionate, intelligent cat that, despite its lack of a tail, is a good hunter. Reputed to be easy to train.

Origin: An ancient breed with many legends as to its origin. It has been said that the first Manx had its tail bitten off by a dog while a passenger in Noah's Ark; also that a Manx swam ashore from a ship of the Spanish Armada. A book, written 200 years ago, is lodged in the Manx Museum, Isle of Man, referring to the tail-less cats of the Island, where there is indeed a state cattery.

Grooming: Use a medium-sized brush and a medium-toothed comb.

Breeding: Difficult to breed, particularly as kittens with normal tails are likely to occur in litters due to inheritance of two genes for a normal tail.

Colouring: All colours and coat patterns acceptable. There are some exclusions in the US, for instance, chocolate, lavender and Himalayan colours; also patterns of those colours with white.

Desired qualities: The stumpy Manx, with a short tail 'stump' is ineligible from exhibition in most countries. Desired is the 'rumpy' which ideally has a dimple where its tail should – or would – be.

Drawbacks: Spina bifida is relatively common.

Oriental Blue

Characteristics: See Oriental Shorthair. Affectionate, intelligent, and a great escapologist.

Origin: These foreign blues now have their own show standard. They were for some time overlooked because of their similarity to other blues. They are the product of Havanas (Self Browns) and Oriental Lilacs.

Grooming: Comb daily. Rub down with a silk handkerchief or chamois leather.

Breeding: See Oriental Shorthair. They occur naturally in litters referred to.

Colouring: Light – to medium-blue from root of coat to tip. Eyes, green.

Desired qualities: See Oriental Shorthair.

Drawbacks: None known.

Oriental Cinnamon

Characteristics: See Oriental Shorthair.

Origin: Developed from a seal-point Siamese, with gene for chocolate, mated to a Red Abyssinian. It is a lighter shade than the Havana, but very similar.

Grooming: Daily combing. Rubbing with a silk handkerchief or chamois leather, will make the coat shine.

Breeding: Prolific breeders.

Colouring: Warm, milk chocolate brown from root to tail. Green eyes.

Desired qualities: See Havana. No white hairs or tabby markings.

Drawbacks: None known.

Oriental Cream

Characteristics: See Oriental Shorthair. Affectionate, intelligent will roam if given the chance.

Origin: When Oriental Blues and Lilacs were first produced, British Shorthaired Tortoiseshells were mated to Siamese. Various solid colours resulted. Genetically, Cream is a dilute of the Red.

Grooming: Comb daily. Rub down with a silk handkerchief or chamois leather.

Breeding: See Oriental Shorthair.

Colouring: Buff Cream. Eyes, green, but copper allowed.

Desired qualities: See Oriental Shorthair.

Drawbacks: None known.

Oriental Ebony (Foreign Black)

Characteristics: See Oriental Shorthair. Affectionate, intelligent. Hates to be confined.

Origin: Prior to the 1970s, the occasional Black Oriental had appeared and been sold to the pet market. The variety did not have a show standard. In the 1970s they were purposely bred by mating Havanas (Self Browns) to Sealpoint Siamese.

Grooming: Comb daily. Rub down with a silk handkerchief or chamois leather..

Breeding: See Oriental Shorthair. Outcrossing is no longer necessary.

Colouring: Jet black coat from root to tip. Emerald green eyes.

Desired qualities: See Oriental Shorthair.

Drawbacks: None known. Need companionship and warmth.

Oriental Lilac

Characteristics: See Oriental Shorthair.

Origin: Developed in the United Kingdom during the Havana breeding programme. Nowadays, Lilac studs should be sufficiently plentiful for outcrossing to be obsolete. However the mating of two brown Havanas will produce Lilac kittens 'where the parents were the progeny of a Russian Blue and a Sealpoint Siamese'.

Grooming: Daily combing. Rubbing with a silk handkerchief, or chamois leather will make the coat shine.

Breeding: Prolific breeders.

Colouring: A pinky-grey coat, the frosty grey tone of which should be neither too blue, nor too fawn. Eyes, green.

Desired qualities: See Oriental Shorthair.

Drawbacks: None known.

Oriental Red

Characteristics: See Oriental Shorthair. Affectionate, intelligent and a great escapologist.

Origin: A by-product of Siamese Red-point breeding in the days when red tabby shorthairs were crossed with Siamese to introduce the red-point colour. Now produced by mating Oriental Blacks to Red-point Siamese.

Grooming: Comb daily. Rub down with a silk handkerchief or chamois leather.

Breeding: See Oriental Shorthair. The Oriental Red is not easy to breed without tabby markings.

Colouring: Brilliant red without markings or shading. Eyes, preferably green; copper allowed.

Desired qualities: See Oriental Shorthair.

Drawbacks: None known.

Oriental Self Brown

The head of the Oriental Self is not so rounded as that of the American Havana Brown.

Characteristics: See Havana Brown.

Origin: The first all-brown, short-haired cat was exhibited in England in 1894. It was billed as the Swiss Mountain cat and thought to have resulted from the accidental mating of a seal-point Siamese and a pet black shorthair. It did not catch on. However the cat type known, in England, as Havana has been bred since the 1950s, resulting from the planned mating of a chocolate-point Siamese and a domestic shorthair of oriental type. It is called Havana because its colour resembles that of Havana tobacco.

Grooming: Daily combing. Rubbing with a silk handkerchief, or chamois leather will make the coat shine.

Breeding: Prolific breeders.

Colouring: Chestnut-brown, the colour of Havana tobacco.

Desired qualities: See Havana and Siamese.

Drawbacks: None known.

Oriental Shorthair (Foreign Shorthair)

Characteristics: A beautiful and affectionate cat that is good with children and dogs, easy to look after, and revels in family life – and warmth.

Origin: Orientals must conform to the same body standard as the Siamese and it is interesting that the original Siamese were not, in their native home, restricted to 'the points'. However, the first cats from Thailand (Siam) to attract attention were indeed pointed. In fact, Oriental Shorthairs resulted from the matings of Siamese and other shorthaired cats for colour, and later with Chinchillas to produce tipped coats.

Grooming: Daily combing. Rubbing with a silk handkerchief, or chamois leather will make the coat shine.

Breeding: Prolific breeders.

Colouring: There is a very wide selection of colours.

Desired qualities: See Siamese.

Drawbacks: None known, but do need warmth and will roam if given the chance.

Oriental Self Colours (other solid shades)

Characteristics: See Oriental Shorthair. Affectionate, intelligent. Will roam, if given the chance.

Origin: When the Shaded Oriental Shorthairs were being developed, the mating occurred of a male Siamese and a Chinchilla Persian queen. In turn their progeny were mated to Redpoint Siamese so as to introduce other colours. During the process a number of colours were produced which are still experimental, cannot be readily reproduced, and do not, as yet, have a show standard. They include Caramel, Apricot and Beige.

Grooming: Comb daily. Rub down with a silk handkerchief or chamois leather.

Breeding: See Oriental Shorthair.

Colouring: See Origin.

Desired qualities: See Oriental Shorthair.

Drawbacks: Not as yet reliably produced.

Oriental Shaded

Characteristics: See Oriental Shorthair. Affectionate, intelligent. Likes its freedom.

Origin: Like the Oriental Tipped, the Shaded variety was developed from a Siamese-Chinchilla mating, the progeny being mated back to Siamese, Oriental Blacks or Havanas. Once the desired effect had been achieved, selective breeding took place.

Grooming: Comb daily. Rub down with a silk handkerchief or chamois leather.

Breeding: See Oriental Shorthair.

Colouring: Undercoat should be pure white. The tipping on back, flanks, head and tail, should be sufficient to resemble a mantle resting on the white coat. Eyes, usually green, but vary with tipping.

Desired qualities: See Oriental Shorthair.

Drawbacks: None known.

Oriental Smoke

Characteristics: See Oriental Shorthair. Affectionate, intelligent and a great escapologist.

Origin: Another by-product of Siamese and Chinchilla-Persian mating, the first example being the offspring of an Oriental Shaded Silver and a Red-point Siamese.

Grooming: Comb daily. Rub down with a silk handkerchief or chamois leather.

Breeding: See Oriental Shorthair. Oriental Smokes are still bred back to Siamese, Havanas and Oriental Blacks to preserve type.

Colouring: There are a number of colours including, black, blue, lilac cameo, chocolate and also tortoiseshell in brown, blue, chocolate and lilac.

Desired qualities: White undercoat. Top coat tipped with contrasting colour. Tipping should be such that, when at rest, the cat appears to be of the tipped colour.

Drawbacks: None known.

Oriental Tabby

Characteristics: See Oriental Shorthair. Affectionate, intelligent. Dislikes being confined.

Origin: Tabby Oriental Shorthairs came about during initial breeding of the Tabby-point (or Lynx) Siamese. At that time, pet Tabbies were used with Siamese. Later, Havanas were mated to Tabby-point Siamese.

Grooming: Comb daily. Rub down with a silk handkerchief or chamois leather.

Breeding: See Origin. It should be noted that, in the UK, Spotted Tabbies were at one time called Egyptian Maus. The original name has now been restored so as to avoid confusion with the American-bred Egyptian Mau.

Colouring: All colours and tabby patterns are acceptable. These are numerous, including, the Mackerel Tabby pattern, Spotted Tabby, Ticked Tabby, Brown, Blue, Chocolate, Lilac, Red, Cream, Silver and Cameo Oriental Tabby.

Desired qualities: See Oriental Shorthair.

Drawbacks: None known.

Oriental Tipped

Characteristics: See Oriental shorthair. Affectionate, intelligent. Will roam if given the chance.

Origin: A Siamese was mated to a Chinchilla Persian with the aim of producing oriental cats with the tipped coat pattern. For a time the progeny were mated back to Siamese but they now breed true with the desired coat pattern.

Grooming: Comb daily. Rub down with a silk handkerchief or chamois leather.

Breeding: See Oriental Shorthair.

Colouring: Tipping similar to that of the British Tipped Shorthair, and in any colour, including, cameo, cameo tabby, blue, silver, chestnut, lilac; also tortoiseshell in brown, blue, lilac and chestnut.

Desired qualities: See Oriental Shorthair. The undercoat should be snow white; the top coat very slightly tipped on the back, flanks, head and tail with a contrasting colour. Eyes, usually green, but vary according to colour of tipping.

Drawbacks: None known.

Oriental Tortie (Patched Tabby)

Characteristics: See Oriental Shorthair. Affectionate, intelligent and will wander if the chance occurs.

Origin: This variety appeared at the time when Oriental Tipped were being produced. They evolved during the breeding programme in litters from matings between Shaded Silver Orientals and Red-point Siamese.

Grooming: Comb daily. Rub down with a silk handkerchief or chamois leather.

Breeding: See Origin.

Colouring: Brown, with patches of red, silver or chocolate; tabby with patches of red; blue or lilac with patches of cream. Eyes, green preferred.

Desired qualities: Nose leather and pad of paws to be patched with the relevant solid colour.

Drawbacks: None known.

Oriental Torties (Particolour)

Characteristics: See Oriental Shorthair. Affectionate, intelligent. Dislike being confined.

Origin: A female-only variety derived from Red and Cream Oriental Shorthairs. It has been recorded that they were originally produced by mating Oriental Blacks with Redpoint Siamese, or Havanas with Red-point Siamese. These days they are obtained by mating Oriental Torties to Siamese, or indeed other Oriental Shorthairs, of solid colours.

Grooming: Comb daily. Rub down with a silk handkerchief or chamois leather.

Breeding: See Origin: See also Oriental Shorthair.

Colouring: May be Brown Tortie, Blue Tortie, Chestnut Tortie or Lilac-cream Tortie.

Desired qualities: In the case of Brown, the coat should be black with unbrindled patches of red and cream; Blue should have blue coat with patches of solid cream; Chestnut should be chestnut brown with unbrindled patches of red and cream; Lilac-cream should be lilac-grey with patches of solid cream.

Drawbacks: None known.

Oriental White (Foreign White)

Characteristics: See Oriental Shorthair. Affectionate, intelligent, and a great escapologist.

Origin: Developed in the 1960s and 1970s by mating white domestic shorthairs to Siamese. they were again later outcrossed to perpetuate the Siamese eye colour.

Grooming: Comb daily. Rub down with a silk handkerchief or chamois leather.

Breeding: Prolific breeders. Kittens can be susceptible to disease. Best to inoculate early.

Colouring: Pure white coat. No black hairs. Eyes should be blue, green allowed in the USA.

Desired qualities: See Oriental Shorthair.

Drawbacks: None known. Need companionship and warmth.

Peke-Faced Persian

Characteristics: A dog-faced cat! Quiet, loving and ideal for apartment living. Does need a great deal of care.

Origin: A longhaired Persian, recognised only in the United States, and developed from Red Self and Tabby longhairs with heavy jowls. Its nose resembles that of the Pekingese dog. It has been exhibited in North America since the 1930s, but is relatively unknown elsewhere.

Grooming: Daily brushing and combing. Remove any mucous that forms in the corner of the eyes.

Breeding: Peke-faced cats do not necessarily breed true. There is a high mortality rate among kittens because of the variety's breathing – and sometimes feeding – problems. Those with less pronounced Peke features are likely to be much healthier.

Colouring: Red, and Red tabby.

Desired qualities: A cobby, Persian-type cat with a Pekingese face and almost bulging, round, full eyes.

Drawbacks: Its breathing structure can lead to problems and trouble with tear ducts. Because of this there is some controversy whether the variety should be perpetuated. It is extremely rare.

Ragdoll

Characteristics: Large and cuddly. Suitable for apartment living and reputed to be impervious to pain.

Origin: Originated in California with kittens born to a white Persian queen who had been injured in a road accident. The breed is said to be impervious to pain and some say this is a throwback to the original queen. However this is against all genetic principles. More likely a white Angora, a Birman and a non-pedigree Burmese formed the foundation stock resulting in a large, vigorous type that breeds true.

Grooming: Daily grooming, using a wide-toothed comb, then a long-bristled brush. This breed requires work if its coat is not to become matted.

Breeding: Ragdoll should be mated to Ragdoll. Kittens are born white, point colours and shading developing gradually. They are slow to mature.

Colouring: There are three coat patterns, bicolour, colourpoint and mitted, and in seal–, chocolate–, blue–and lilac-point within these patterns.

Desired qualities: A large, cuddly cat with a flowing coat and a tendency to go limp when held.

Drawbacks: None known except that high pain tolerance might lead it into danger.

Red Persian

Characteristics: Most beautiful, quiet and affectionate cat. Will easily adapt to apartment life.

Origin: While 'ginger' cats are almost always male, it is possible to produce red females by mating the red tom with a tortoiseshell or blue-cream female.

Grooming: Daily brushing and combing. An application of bay rum will make the coat shine.

Breeding: Kittens are invariably born with tabby markings which may, or may not, disappear as the kittens develop. Producing clear reds is not easy.

Colouring: Rich, deep red without any white hairs or other markings. Eyes, deep copper.

Desired qualities: Brick red nose leather and paw pads.

Drawbacks: Moults. A gentle cat that does not appreciate being teased.

Rex (Si-Rex)

Characteristics: Unusual, curly-coated cat with great sense of fun. Affectionate, intelligent and can be trained to the lead.

Origin: See Cornish Rex and Devon Rex.

Grooming: One of the easiest of cats to look after. A rub down with a silk handkerchief or chamois leather is all that is necessary.

Breeding: The Si-Rex is obtained by mating a Rex to a Siamese, which introduces the Himalayan coat pattern.

Colouring: All colour and coat patterns acceptable, including Himalayan. The eyes of the Si-Rex should be blue.

Desired qualities: See Cornish Rex and Devon Rex.

Drawbacks: None known.

Russian Blue

Characteristics: Possibly the ideal companion: affectionate, beautiful, silent and shy. It has a short, dense coat like sealskin, adapts well to apartment living, and can sometimes be trained to harness and lead.

Origin: Originally known as the Archangel Blue, the first imports, Lingpop and Yula, both came from Archangel on the North-west Russian coast.

Grooming: Occasional brushing and combing with a fine-toothed comb. Polish with a chamois leather. Stroking helps too.

Breeding: Because of the scarcity of breed members the Russian Blue was, to its detriment, outcrossed with British Blue and Blue-point Siamese at the end of the nineteenth century. Since World War II better specimens are being produced. But finding suitable breeding stock is still a problem. Queens usually have only one or two litters a year.

Colouring: Clear, all over blue with no shading or white hairs. However silver-tipped guard hairs give the coat a silvery sheen. Medium blue preferred. A paler shade is liked in the United States.

Desired qualities: A short, thick, silvery-blue coat of a sealskin texture. Dainty build. Small head, green eyes and vertical ears.

Drawbacks: Possibly its quiet voice. It might not be heard, if shut in somewhere.

Scottish Fold

Characteristics: Very unusual. Best described as the French Bulldog of the cat world because of its distinctive bat-like ears. Affectionate, with a 'large' personality and fondness for humans and other animals.

Origin: Appeared as a natural mutation in a farm litter, in Scotland, in 1961. William Ross, a shepherd, recognised uniqueness when 'Susie', one of the 'Fold' kittens, produced similar progeny two years later. A breeding programme began which caused delight in some circles, dismay in others where upright and pricked ears are preferred.

Grooming: Daily brushing and combing.

Breeding: Mated to a normal shorthaired domestic cat the progeny will be 50% Fold. The variety cannot be registered in the UK, where it was feared that the breed might be subject to ear mites and deafness. It is popular in North America.

Colouring: Almost unlimited. Eye colour must be in keeping with coat.

Desired qualities: Folded ears, like those of a puppy, and an accompanying 'sad' expression. A preference for small, tightly folded ears rather than large, more loosely folded ones.

Drawbacks: Ineligibility to exhibit and difficulty in finding.

Shaded Persian

Characteristics: Most beautiful, quiet and affectionate cat. Will easily adapt to apartment life.

Origin: Frequently appear in Chinchilla and Cameo litters. More popular in the United States than the United Kingdom, but some attractive shades are being introduced. (See Cameo and Chinchillas.)

Grooming: Daily brushing and combing. An application of bay rum will make the coat shine.

Breeding: See Cameos and Chinchilla.

Colouring: May be shaded silver, cameo, pewter, golden or tortoiseshell. The undercoat should be pure white except in the case of the golden, when it should be cream.

Desired qualities: See also Shell Cameo and Chinchilla.

Drawbacks: Moults.

Shell Cameo Persian

Characteristics: A very beautiful cat, the hardiness of which belies its daintiness and mystical expression.

Origin: First selectively bred in the United States in the mid-1960s and fast gaining popularity. The Shell Cameo is very similar to the Chinchilla. The Cameo factor is derived by mating a silver to a red-gened cat, or its dilute form, cream.

Grooming: Bath about a week before a show, then powder daily to restore the coat's body. Comb to prevent tangles. The coat should be fluffy, with each hair standing out. Make sure all traces of powder are removed.

Breeding: See Origin. Kittens are born white.

Colouring: Like the Chinchilla the Cameo may be Smoke and Shaded Silver, with red tipping instead of black. Undercoat should be white, eyes copper.

Desired qualities: Cobby, well-coupled cat with short, firm legs, large round–, copper-coloured eyes, and long, dense silky coat with long full frill.

Drawbacks: Needs lots of grooming.

Siamese

Characteristics: Affectionate, demanding, elegant, talkative and intelligent. Arguably the most dog-like of cats and can be trained to the lead.

Origin: The best-known, most popular pure-bred cat whose history has been lost in antiquity. Undoubtedly the breed existed in Thailand (then called Siam) for several hundred years prior to examples being exhibited at Crystal Palace, London in 1885. These exhibits are believed to have been presented to the British consul by the King of Siam. In those days, Siamese were famous for their kinked tails and squint eyes. These faults have now been bred out.

Grooming: Easy to look after. Enjoy being brushed and combed. Usually keep themselves spotless. If they don't, it could be a sign of ill-health.

Breeding: Prolific breeders. Kittens are born white. Points develop gradually.

Colouring: Seal-point is the best-known colour, but points may be chocolate, blue, lilac and other shades, (see Colourpoint).

Desired qualities: Vivid blue eyes. Points of required colour on mask, ears, legs and tail. A cat that is slim, lithe and muscular.

Drawbacks: Absolutely none, unless you dislike a strong, determined personality.

Singapura

Characteristics: A small, quiet, robust cat that is responsive to affection. It has distinctive, large, cupped ears, and loves eating fish!

Origin: Referred to by some as 'just an alley cat' the Singapura is a natural breed that inhabits the 'drains' of Singapore. However, it does have a competition standard. Many Singapuras, admired by travellers, found their way to the United States, where they were first exhibited in 1977.

Grooming: Very little. Occasional combing.

Breeding: Few problems. However, neither male nor female mate until they are eighteen months of age and kittens are slow to mature.

Colouring: Ticked ivory and brown coats and golden eyes.

Desired qualities: A very small cat with a fine, short, silky coat, large, almond-shaped eyes and a medium-length tail tapering to a blunt tip, without any kinks.

Drawbacks: None known. But may be a little timid until its confidence has been gained.

Small wild cat(s): European/African

Characteristics: Of the two varieties named, only the African wild cat would seem to have been tamed. Its mummified remains have been found, signifying its pet status with the Ancient Egyptians.

Origin: The African wild cat comes from the open woodlands of Africa and South-east Asia. Other small wild cats, all of which are closely related, include the Black-footed cat from South Africa, the Chinese Desert cat, the Jungle cat of Southern Asia, the Sand cat from North Africa and the Leopard cat from Western Asia. The European wild cat is rarely seen, except in the Highlands of Scotland. It is distinguishable from the domestic cat by its larger skull and teeth and its tail, which is rounded at the tip.

Breeding: Not selectively bred.

Colouring: The African wild cat has tabby markings, its basic colour ranging from grey to tawny yellow. The European wild cat has large tabby markings.

Desired qualities: The African wild cat stand 35cm (14in) high at the shoulder, larger than domestic cats.

Drawbacks: These cats are not pets.

Smoke Persian

Characteristics: Most beautiful, quiet and affectionate cat. Will easily adapt to apartment life.

Origin: Smokes were first recorded in the United Kingdom in the 1860s when they appeared in litters of Chinchillas, Black, Blue and White Persians. They are now purpose-bred in various shades but have not yet attained universal show status.

Grooming: Daily brushing and combing. An application of bay rum will make the coat shine.

Breeding: Frequent mating of Smoke to Smoke results in loss of Persian type. Outcrossing can be to black, blue or tortoiseshell Persians provided the parents have smoke ancestry. But is a chancy business.

Colouring: Currently may be black, blue, cameo or tortoiseshell smoke, with other colours likely to be introduced.

Desired qualities: The tipped colour should appear to be a self colour until the cat moves and the undercoat is apparent.

Drawbacks: None known. Relatively rare.

Snowshoe

Characteristics: A sometimes noisy, amiable cat of extreme rarity and unusual appearance.

Origin: The Snowshoe was produced by mating the Siamese with bicolour American shorthairs. It has the characteristics of both types. Selective breeding is taking place, and it has been accepted as a provisional breed, without championship status, in Britain.

Grooming: Normal brushing and combing. Stroking improves coat.

Breeding: Siamese, and any solid-coloured Himalayan patterned cat may be used. In Britain pedigrees may also include Bi-coloured British or European shorthair.

Colouring: The Snowshoe should have white and coloured points, ie, snowshoes!

Desired qualities: A shorthaired Birman-patterned cat, but with a head longer than would be liked in that variety. Eyes are vivid blue. Hind and forefeet, white. White inverted 'V' on muzzle.

Drawbacks: A rarity even in North America, but interest is developing.

Somali (Longhaired Abyssinian)

Characteristics: Gentle, affectionate and quiet, it is playful, easy to groom, and makes a good family pet.

Origin: Most Somalis can be traced back to Abyssinians in the UK that were mated to longhaired cats. However, certain Abyssinian breeding lines are now known to have carried the recessive gene for long hair for many generations. In the late 1960s efforts were made to develop the longhaired Abyssinian under the name Somali. Popular in North America, it does not have show status in the UK at the time of writing.

Grooming: Easy to groom. The coat does not usually mat. Use a medium-toothed comb.

Breeding: Breeds true. May also appear in Abyssinian litters where both sides carry the recessive gene for long hair.

Colouring: Ruddy and Red. Kittens in the former shade are born quite dark, the ticked coat taking a long time to develop. The red colour is a warm, glowing shade, ticked with chocolate-brown.

Desired qualities: The Somali should look like the Abyssinian except for its coat, which should be sufficiently long to show numerous bands of ticking.

Drawbacks: None known.

Sphynx

Characteristics: A hairless cat, the body of which is warm and smooth to the touch. Affectionate and good natured, it is not susceptible to the cold.

Origin: The Canadians have taken an interest in this breed since, in 1966, a hairless kitten was born to a Black and White Domestic Shorthair in Ontario. Hairless kittens have also appeared in litters of ordinary Shorthairs, and other breeds, in the United Kingdom and France. The Aztecs are known to have had hairless cats, some of which were recorded in Mexico at the end of the nineteenth century.

Grooming: No brushing or combing. The dander which accumulates on the skin must be sponged with warm water.

Breeding: Sphynx cats breed true. They are born with a fine veil of soft, short hair, which disappears in adulthood. Kittens are bow-legged and have wrinkled, loose skins.

Colouring: All colour and coat patterns (see American Wirehair) except the Himalayan pattern, chocolate, lilac (lavender) or any of these with white.

Desired qualities: Medium-sized, fine-boned, but powerful.

Drawbacks: None known. Might not appeal to those with an aversion to reptiles.

Tabby Persian

Characteristics: Beautiful, affectionate, quiet, but possibly more adventurous than other Persian varieties.

Origin: Longhaired tabbies were first recorded in Europe at the end of the sixteenth century. It would appear from the markings of wild cats that probably the original tabby was striped, similar to the Mackeral Tabby. The blotched pattern, common in feral and domestic cats, was quite common as early as the seventeenth century, although selective breeding has now produced colours other than the likely brown or ginger.

Grooming: See Tortoiseshell Persian.

Breeding: Breed true. Sensible to outcross after several generation. Kittens show markings from birth.

Colouring: Brown tabbies are attractive but difficult to produce. Other colours include red, silver, blue, cream, cameo, and patched tabby in brown, silver and blue.

Desired qualities: See Tabby. Even rings on legs and tail

Drawbacks: None known, except the need for constant brushing.

Tiffany

Characteristics: See Burmese. A good natured, playful cat of high intelligence. Easily trained to walk on a lead.

Origin: The Tiffany is, in fact, a longhaired Burmese. It is purposebred in North America, but rare in the United Kingdom.

Grooming: Brushing and combing.

Breeding: Percentage possibly Birman and Burmese.

Colouring: Kittens are born with blue eyes. They become grey then golden. Coat colour, café au lait changing to Burmese brown.

Desired qualities: A longhaired Burmese that combines silky, long hair with the shaded brown tones of the Burmese.

Drawbacks: None known, but virtually impossible to obtain.

Tonkinese

Characteristics: Active and affectionate with insatiable curiosity and little, or no, fear. Adores people and can sometimes be trained to harness and lead.

Origin: A cross between two popular breeds, the Siamese and the Burmese, the 'Tonk' was developed in the 1960s and 1970s in the United States and Canada. It has the inherited characteristics of both ancestors along with their devotion to people and curious nature. Because of their strong inclination to be with humans, they are, alas, sometimes involved in road accidents; therefore owners may decide to provide an escape-free run, if they go to work. But don't confine this free spirit to a small area!

Grooming: Use a fine-toothed comb and rub down with a silk cloth or chamois leather. Regular stroking.

Breeding: The first cross of Siamese to Burmese produces 100% Tonkinese. It is early days yet for this breed.

Colouring: Five expensive-sounding colours are allowed: natural mink, honey mink, champagne mink, blue mink and platinum mink.

Desired qualities: An oriental-type cat, medium-sized, lithe and well-muscled.

Drawbacks: Its propensity to wander.

Tortoiseshell Persian

Characteristics: Beautiful, affectionate, quiet. Easily adapts to apartment life.

Origin: Despite the popularity of shorthaired tortoiseshells, longhaired torties did not appear until the early 1900s.

Grooming: Daily brushing and combing.

Breeding: This is a female-only variety and difficult to breed. Producing a good Tortoiseshell Persian is more by luck than skill. Mating self coloured males does not always produce the desired effect. Tabby sires should not be used. This begets undesirable markings.

Colouring: A coat that is evenly patched with red, cream and black, in which black should not predominate. Eyes, copper or deep orange.

Desired qualities: Colours should be broken up on head and ears. There should not be large patches of any one colour. A blaze from forehead to nose is not liked.

Drawbacks: These cats are rare and therefore tend to be expensive.

Tortoiseshell and White Persian (Calico)

Characteristics: Beautiful, affectionate, quiet. Easily adapts to apartment life.

Origin: Although shorthaired, tortoiseshell and white cats have been around for centuries, one can only surmise how the longhaired variety appeared, possibly in litters of Persians of solid colour with mixed colour background. It is a colour that is applicable to females only. Where a male does appear, usually it is sterile.

Grooming: Daily brushing and combing.

Breeding: Such cats are often born when sired by red and white, or black and white, bicoloured cats. Tabbies should not be used.

Colouring: The cat should be patched with black, red and cream, intermingled with white.

Desired qualities: Patches should be equally distributed without white hairs or tabby markings. (In this, as in several other cases, the American shown standard differs slightly from that in the United Kingdom.)

Drawbacks: None known. A popular variety.

Turkish Van Cat

Characteristics: An unusual, hardy and intelligent cat that is renowned for its love of water, and its ability to swim. NB: There are also Van Persians. These are usually white with colour patches on head, legs and tail.

Origin: Believed to have originated through interbreeding in a specific geographical area, the Van region of Turkey. The variety has been known for centuries. They were introduced into the United Kingdom in the 1950s.

Grooming: Daily combing. Bath this cat if you want to, but mind that it does not catch cold.

Breeding: Breed true. No need for outcrossing.

Colouring: Chalk white with auburn markings on face and around, and underneath ears. There should be a white blaze between the ears, nose, cheeks and chin.

Desired qualities: See Colouring. Tail is ringed in two shades of auburn. Eyes, pale amber.

Drawbacks: None known, but relatively rare and expensive. Moults in spring and summer.

White Persian (Odd-Eyed White)

Characteristics: Beautiful, affectionate, quiet. Ideally suited to apartment life.

Origin: One of the oldest varieties, long regarded as a status symbol. Known in Europe for 300 years, but earlier Whites had longer faces, blue eyes and were invariably deaf. There are three varieties: Blue-eyed White, Orange-eyed White and the Odd-eyed White which has an eye of each colour. The Odd-eyed White is most appealing, but the cat may often be deaf on the blue-eyed side.

Grooming: Daily brushing and combing. Talcum, or grooming powder, brushed through coat.

Breeding: Breed true. All kittens are born with blue eyes, so it can be some weeks before the breeder can tell which of the three varieties the offspring will be.

Colouring: Pure white (no markings).

Desired qualities: The typical cobby body, short tail and broad head of the Persian cat.

Drawbacks: Owning a deaf cat can be a problem. Frequently it is unaware of danger.

Choice and Care

What type of cat should one choose? There is nothing more noble than to rush out and offer a home to a cat, or kitten, that is facing destruction, and organisations such as The Cats Protection League are always in need of homes for misplaced moggies. However, all too often owners acquiring a pet on impulse realise thereafter the choice that would have been open to them had they taken the time, and trouble, to buy a book like this beforehand and study the pictures and descriptions.

Even when buying a pedigree kitten purchasers may, in their enthusiasm, omit to mention that they would like to enter it in shows, or proceed under the misapprehension that, because the animal has a certificate of pedigree, it must be a show prospect. This is a common mistake. The certificate proves that the animal is the progeny of parents of the same variety whose line is traceable for several generations. It may be a happy, healthy pretty cat. However, its marking, size, or some other factor may rule it out for a show career. If you want a show prospect ask the breeder to pick one out for you, or take a knowledgeable fancier along with you when you go to make your choice.

There are a number of publications in the United Kingdom and overseas (see p 133-135) which list breeders of the cat varieties. Information can also be obtained by sending a self-addressed stamped envelope to the Governing Council of the Cat Fancy or, for example, the American Cat Fanciers Association.

Shorthaired
or longhaired

Do you want a cat with short or long hair? Most cat- and dog-lovers, seem to have a definite preference for short- or long-coated animals. It is true that cats are scrupulously clean animals that wash their own fur. However, they require regular grooming, and the long coat will require that bit of extra time and attention and could be guilty of depositing a few extra hairs on the carpet. This is particularly noticeable in the case of white cats.

Feeding and Housing

First of all let me disprove the old adage that you should not feed a farm cat because it will grow lazy and disinclined to catch mice – and that the suburban pet cat should be put out at night.

Both suppositions are rubbish. In the first place the cat that is well-fed is more likely to be a proficient hunter than that which is under-nourished, while it is cruel in the extreme to remove a feline from a warm fireside, putting it out into the night where it might be injured, get lost, or be stolen. Worse, it might be picked up by some unscrupulous person intent on collecting cats to sell to vivisection laboratories.

Let your cat sleep by the fireside in a basket, perhaps lined with synthetic sheepskin material, and possibly invest in a cat flap so that your pet may go in and out at will. Let it be said that there are many cats that live in apartments, quite contentedly, use litter trays, and never see the outside world. Remember, however, that cats do need to eat grass. This is a natural medicine for relieving bile and sourness. It also acts as an emitic and is the means of inducing the vomiting of hairballs. Cocksfoot grass can be obtained in seed pots from the Cats Protection League and other sources.

Most likely your kitten will, when you collect it, be about eight weeks of age – it should not be less than six weeks. By then it should be able to eat a quarter- to a half-can of branded kitten food per day or maybe, if you prefer, the same quantity of cooked fish, minced meat or rabbit, either plain, or mixed with brown bread and barley.

Nowadays most busy owners prefer to feed on prepared branded products which contain all the nutritional requirements of the animal, and which have been scientifically prepared. A grown cat might need a can, roughly 182-189g (6½-6¾oz), but it could require half this amount again if it is a large, particularly active, hungry cat. Alternatively, you might 'serve' a complete cat food containing energy food as well as meat, fish or liver. There are also convenient soft, moist foods which provide a balanced diet, and complete dry feeds which may be moistened with water or milk. If you do feed a complete dry preparation you must make sure that your cat has an ample supply of drinking water or milk. Please keep water available at ALL times. Some cats adore milk, others prefer water. And, incidentally, please do not offer liver, except as an occasional treat. It is far too rich for the cat's digestion and acts as a purgative.

The kitten, since weaning, will have received several feeds each day, divided into two meat meals and two milky meals, for instance, baby food such as Farex, Complan or baby rice, mixed with evaporated milk. Never stint a hungry kitten!

You may gradually reduce the number of feeds given until it is receiving one meaty meal a day when it is about nine months of age. Some owners prefer to divide this feed into two meals, given at different times of the day. But, whichever system you choose, stick to it, and do not deviate from the selected feeding time(s).

Training

Cats are naturally clean animals and your kitten will quickly learn the purpose of the litter tray. Place the pet on to it after each meal – or mistake. Even small kittens are intelligent!

Once puss is old enough to go outside, the tray can be discarded – unless you intend that it should be a permanent fixture. But whatever you decide, you must ensure that the tray is kept disinfected and that the litter is changed daily. Never clean with carbolic. This, like creosote, is dangerous to cats.

A problem that many owners have is that of the cat, or kitten, sharpening its claws on the furnishings. However, there are numerous cat scratching posts on the market, some in such attractive designs that one is proud to give them pride of place in one's living room. Once you have christened your kitten, use the chosen name whenever you wish to attract the pet's attention: 'Does Tommy want his dinner?' 'Tommy. Come here!' Before long your kitten will associate with the name and come running whenever it hears your call.

Health

Cats are generally long-lived and healthy. My last Siamese lived to a respectable fifteen years. Some cats may live to twenty years or more, others reach the end of their span at twelve years. In the same manner as humans, one individual may live longer than another.

The cat has great self-curative powers and will often heal itself, creeping away to hide until some wound has healed, or eating grass to help itself vomit. However, if you have cause to think that your cat is unwell, please do not hesitate to take it to the veterinary surgery for a check up. Often people fail to do this thinking that their concern may be making a mountain out of a molehill, or that the cost of treatment is prohibitive. Bear in mind that it could be far-more expensive if you fail to have treated promptly a condition which might well have been nipped in the bud.

Most important is that your kitten should be inoculated against infectious feline enteritis, the most serious of cat diseases and, likewise, cat flu and feline distemper. There is often some variance in the age at which veterinarians like to administer jabs, so do check with your surgery.

Unless you are planning to breed cats on a commercial basis, it is vitally important that a tom (male) cat should be neutered (or doctored) and a queen (female) cat spayed.

The queen comes into season every three or four weeks in summer, and there are never enough homes for the kittens to go round, while the tom, if unneutered, is a compulsive fighter and will inevitably become battle scarred if left undoctored. Indeed he may become severely injured if, in later years, he is set upon by a younger, stronger male. After neutering the tom loses the desire to fight and becomes a more loving and homely companion; also he does not smell so antisocial for, alas, all unneutered toms tend to spray, leaving an unmistakable 'catty' odour.

Holidays

Once you become a cat owner, arrangements must be made for your pet when you go away on holiday, or even if you need to be away on business for a day or two.

Maybe you have a neighbour who likes cats and who can be relied upon to pop in to let your cat out several times during the day, and to feed it.

There are, however, many catteries where cats are boarded, usually for a daily charge, by people with sound knowledge of cats. A good establishment will have a veterinarian on call, will enquire as to your cat's usual diet, likes and dislikes; and will insist on seeing an up-to-date inoculation record card and request the telephone number of your own veterinarian and one where you may be contacted, in case of emergency, during the boarding. Possibly your cat's breeders may run such an establishment, or they may be able to recommend one. Alternatively, it is worth enquiring at the veterinary surgery, or at the local pet shop.

Showing

Once you have bought a prospective show kitten, you will no doubt decide to join the relevant breed club, for instance, the Abyssinian Cat Association or the Blue-pointed Siamese Cat Club. This will enable you to learn about the variety, to attend club shows, and to meet other enthusiasts. You may even decide to join the ranks of cat breeders.

In the United Kingdom all pure-bred cats are judged by an official standard approved by the Governing Council of the Cat Fancy. All pure-bred cats which are exhibited have to be registered with the Fancy. Owners receive a Certificate of Pedigree at the time of purchase and subsequently have ownership of the cat officially transferred from the breeder to themselves and recorded by the Fancy on payment of a small fee.

In America the situation is more complicated for there is not a single governing body but eight or more, each of which may have slight differences in its approved standard of points for the perfect cat. But the same general principle applies. That is that the cat must be registered with a governing body before being entered in pure-bred classes.

Cats are judged by a standard of perfection, one hundred marks being those that may be awarded to a perfect example of the type or variety, such marks being given for the exhibit with the right shape of head, ears, body, and fur according to the standard laid down by the official body.

A cat that wins three certificates under three different judges can become a Champion. A cat may become a Grand Champion by winning three Champion Challenge Certificates at three shows under three different judges; but before entering a Grand Champion Class, the exhibit must be a full Champion. Neutered cats can be exhibited in Neuter classes and become what is known as a Premier by winning at three shows under different judges and a Grand Premier under the same rules and conditions as those laid down for a Grand Champion.

In the United Kingdom all pedigree varieties for which there is an official standard also have an allotted breed number. And as breeders enjoy trying to develop cats with, for instance, different colour coat patterns there may be classes for Longhairs AOV (Any other variety), and so on. There is an experimental register for new varieties and a provisional standard, but Championship status is only granted when one hundred breed members have been bred to standard.

Often at a large cat shows there are also classes for pet cats so that the boy or girl with a treasured moggie may have the opportunity of exhibiting it in, say, a class for the best-kept household pet, the best-condition rescued cat, the cat with the most beautiful eyes and so on.

Once you have joined a breed club you will be circularised with details of club shows. However, if you see a show advertised that you would like to enter, you should write to the show secretary asking for a schedule and entry form. Enclose a self-addressed stamped envelope. The schedule will list the classes to be held and you must check in the Definition of Classes those for which your pet is eligible.

Novice classes are open to exhibits that have not won a first prize under GCCF rules, a Limit Class to those that have not won more than four first prizes and so on.

Having sent off your completed entry form and fee you may receive an entry (or tally) number. However you may not be given this until you get to the show, so do not be alarmed if there is no response. If you have any queries, meanwhile, don't be afraid to telephone the secretary. Show officials always give help and encouragement to newcomers.

Methods of showing vary considerably in the United Kingdom and America, so it is suggested that intending exhibitors try to visit a show run under the auspices of the governing body before they make an entry.

Exhibiting cats is not only a fascinating hobby, but one that provides the opportunity to make friends with kindly and interesting people . . . people who love cats just as much as you do.

Information

Addresses of Principal Organisations

The Cats Protection League, 17 Kings Road, Horsham, West Sussex RH13 5PP.

Cat Action Trust, c/o 10 Credo Way, West Thurrock, Essex.

The Governing Council of the Cat Fancy, 4-6 Penel Orlleu, Bridgwater, Somerset TA6 3PG.

The National Cat Club, Greenhayes, 35 Blackwater Lane, Crawley, Sussex RH10 4RN.

Other useful addresses

Abyssinian Cat Association, 65 Preston Drive, Ewell Court, Surrey KT19 0AD.

Abyssinian Cat Club, Abywood, Culmhead, Churchstanton, Taunton, Devon.

The Balinese and Siamese Cat Club, c/o Fairfields, Beech Road, Kessingland, Suffolk.

The Balinese Cat Society, c/o 17 Meadowside, Angmering, West Sussex BN16 4BW.

The Blue-Pointed Siamese Cat Club, 39 The Avenue, Chinor, Oxford, OX9 4PD.

British Ragdoll Club, Brick House, Windmill Hill, East Sussex (or 9 Radbroke Close, Sandbach, Cheshire).

Birmese Cat Club, 11 Eton Avenue, North Finchley, London N12 0BD.

Blue Persian Cat Society, 37 Ryecroft Meadows, Mannings Heath, Horsham, Sussex.

Bucks Oxon and Berks Cat Society, Bridge Lodge, Eythrope Park, Aylesbury, Bucks.

Capital Longhair Cat Association, 8 Parsonage Road, Eastbourne, East Sussex.

Colourpoint Cat Club, 10 Burton Road, Branston, Burton-on-Trent DE14 3DN.

Colourpoint, Rex-coated and AOV Club (Colourpoints, Birmans, Bicolours, Turkish and new cols), 79 Stoney Lane, Bloxwich, Walsall WS3 3ARE.

Colchester and District Cat Rescue and Homing Society, Chesmond Brook Road, Great Tey, Colchester, Essex.

Croydon Cat Club, Silverleigh, Main Road, West Kingsdown, Kent TN15 6EX.

Edinburgh and East of Scotland Cat Club, 1 Hosie Rigg, Edinburgh EH15 3RX.

Foreign Black and Foreign Blue Cat Society, c/o 9 Sedrup Lane, Aylesbury, Bucks.

Foreign White Cat Society, 17 Hall Road, Aughton, Sheffield S31 0XH.

Foreign Cinnamon and Fawn Group, 280 Stanstead Road, Hoddesdon, Herts.

Foreign Blue and Foreign Black Cat Club, Conifers, The Gallop, Sutton, Surrey.

Herts and Middlesex Cat Club, Redleaf, Christ Church Road, Crouch End, London N8 9OL.

Longhair Cream and Blue-cream Association, 21 Third Avenue, Daison, Torquay, Devon.

Longhaired Cat Club, 31 Pickwood, Pickwick Road, London SE21.

Rex Cat Club, 8 Camp Terrace, North Shields, Tyneside NE29 0NE.

Southern Counties Cat Club, Littlecroft, Willow Grove, Chislehurst, Kent.

South Western Counties Cat Club, 16 Gloucester Road, Exwick, Exeter, Devon.

Smoke Cat Society, 15 Parkfield Drive, Ossett, West Yorkshire.

Tabby Colourpoint Cat Club, Ayr, Jigs Lane, Warfield, Bracknell, Berks RG12 6DH.

Wessex Cat Club, 28 Dolphin Avenue, Bournemouth, Hants.

Kit Wilson Trust for Animal Welfare, Rescue Centre, Stonehurst Lane, Hadlow Down, Uckfield, East Sussex TN22 4ED.

If the Club in which you are interested is not listed, please write to the Governing Council of the Cat Fancy, at the address given, enclosing a self-addressed, stamped envelope.

It will be appreciated that while every effort has been made to provide accurate, up-to-date, information, club officials may, in some instances, have changed since we went to press. It is therefore most important that a stamped self-addressed envelope is always enclosed, thus enabling the recipient to pass the letter on, if necessary, to the person for whom it is intended.

New Clubs

The Cat Association of Britain, Mill House, Letcombe Regis, Oxon OX12 9JD.

This Association is a member of the Federation Internationale Feline. FIFe is a non profit making association currently composed of twenty-nine cat fancy organisations worldwide. The Cat Association of Britain was elected a FIFe member in May 1990. The following are the addresses of those clubs that have affiliated to date:

The Aristocats Club, 10 Lyncroft Gardens, Ewell Village, Epsom, Surrey KT17 1UR.

The Burmilla Cat Club, 2 Brentford Close, Cholsey, Oxon OX10 9PZ.

The East Anglia Cat Association, 3 School Common Road, Happisburgh, Norwich, Norfolk NR12 0QF.

The Heart of England Cat Association, 97 Golden Drive, Eaglestone, Milton Keynes, Bucks.

The Sherwood Cat Association, 1 Ellis Avenue, Hucknall, Notts NG15 7RZ.

Snowshoes UK, 10 Lyncroft Gardens, Ewell Village, Epsom, Surrey. (See also Aristocats above.)

The Viking Cat Society, The Bungalow, Main Street, Burton Agnes, East Yorkshire YO25 0NA.

It is understood that the following clubs are working towards affiliation and welcome enquiries:

The Breckland and Broadland Cat Association: Norfolk based: 0379-898053.

The Garden of England Cat Club: Kent based: 0622-858510.

The National Pet Cat Society: Sussex based: 0273-833092.

The National Ragdoll Association: Lincolnshire based: 071-4904000.

The Roses Cat Club: Yorkshire based: 0422-884041.

The Thistle Cat Club: Glasgow based: 0698-282019.

The Tonkinese Breeders Association: Surrey based: 0252-870690.

Should anyone wish to start a new regional club, or a national one, they are warmly invited to contact the Affiliated Clubs Liaison Director, Mrs J. Drury, The Drive, Southwick, Brighton, Sussex BN4 4RR.

Publications

Cats, 5 James Leigh Street, Manchester M1 6EX (Feline weekly. Editor, Brian Doyle).

Cat World (monthly), 10 Western Road, Shoreham-by-Sea, West Sussex BN4 SWD (Editor, Joan Moore).

Kennel and Cattery Management, PO Box 45, Dorking, Surrey RH5 5YZ.

Pedigree Digest, Pedigree Petfoods Ltd, Waltham on the Wolds, Melton Mowbray, Leicestershire LE14 4RS.

Miscellaneous Addresses

Royal Society for the Prevention of Cruelty to Animals (RSPCA), The Causeway, Horsham, Sussex.

Society for Companion Animal Studies (Mrs. Anne Docherty), The Mews Cottage, 7 Botanic Crescent Lane, Glasgow G20 8AA.

And finally . . . Veterinary insurance cover:

DBI PetCover (reference 267825), 9 St. Stephen's Court, St. Stephen's Road, Bournemouth, Hants BH2 6LG.

Bibliography

A Cat of your Own, Dorothy Silkstone Richards (Salamander Books).

Cats, Joan Palmer (Blandford).

Cats and Kittens, Joan Palmer (The Warwick Press).

Cat Watching, Desmond Morris (Jonathan Cape).

Cult of the Cat, Patricia Dale-Green (Heinemann).

The Book of the Cat, Edited by Michael Wright and

Sally Walters (Ward Lock).

The Superbook of Cats, Joan Palmer (Kingfisher Kingpins).

The Observer Book of Cats, Grace Pond (Frederick Warne).

Understanding your Cat, Michael W. Fox (Blond & Briggs).

Overseas addresses

The Cat Fanciers Association Inc. (World's largest pedigreed cat registry), 4517 SE 4th Place, Ocala, Florida 32671.

American Cat Association, 10065 Foothill Boulevard, Lakeview Terrace, California 91342.

American Cat Fanciers Association, PO Box 203, Point Look Out, Missouri 65726.

Canadian Cat Association, 14 Nelson Street West (suite 5), Brampton, Ontario L6X 1BY.

Cat Fanciers' Association, PO Box 430, Red Bank, New Jersey 07701.

Cat Fanciers' Federation, 2013 Elizabeth Street, Schenectady, New York 12303.

Crown Cat Fanciers' Federation, 1379 Tyler Park Drive, Louisville, Kentucky 40204.

Federation Internationale Feline, Friedrichsstrasse, 48. 6200 Wiesbaden, West Germany.

New Zealand Cat Fancy Inc, PO Box 3167, Richmond, Nelson, New Zealand.

The Independent Cat Association, 211 East Olive (Suite 201), Burbank, California 91502.

United Cat Federation, 6621 Thornwood Street, San Diego, California 92111.

also:

American Society for the Prevention of Cruelty to Animals (ASPCA), 441 East 92nd Street, New York NY 10028.

Overseas Publications

All Cats, Pacific Palisadaes, California.

Cat Fancy, PO Box 53264, Boulder, Colorado.

Cats Magazine, Pittsburgh, Pennsylvania.

Cat World, Phoenix, Arizona.

Pet Health News, PO Box 486, Mount Morris, Illinois.

Index of Cat Breeds